Sydney Stadium
Boxing Day 1908

TOM THOMPSON

ETT IMPRINT
Exile Bay

Published by ETT Imprint, Exile Bay in 2025

Copyright in this edition © Tom Thompson 2025

First electronic edition ETT Imprint 2025

This book is copyright. Apart from any fair dealing for the purposes of private study, research, criticism or review, as permitted under the Copyright Act, no part may be reproduced by any process without written permission. Enquiries should be addressed to the publisher via email ettimprint@hotmail com, or in writing to:

ETT IMPRINT
PO Box R1906
Royal Exchange NSW 1225
Australia

ISBN 978-1-923205-52-9 (paper)
ISBN 978-1-923205-53-6 (ebook)

Cover art by Norman Lindsay

Designed by Tom Thompson

The author would like to thank Martin Farrah and Simon Hill at Lawsons Auctions for allowing him to describe and value the John Roberts and Bill O'Loughlin collections, which held most of the rare images in this book.

Contents

Introduction *4*
Tommy Burns - Heavyweight Champion of the World *6*
Jack Johnson - the Coloured Champion *8*
Training Days *13*
Portraits of Tommy Burns by Charles Kerry *16*
Jack Johnson in Sydney 1908 *20*
Norman Lindsay and *The Lone Hand* *22*
Tommy Burns at Medlow Bath *26*
The Souvenir Program and tickets *24*
Sporting Notions *29*
Views of the Stadium - 40
Jack London on the Fight *41*
Boxing Championship - *The Argus* *49*
Johnson and Burns Interviewed *62*
Larry Foley Interviewed *64*
The Burns-Johnson Fight - The Film *65*
An American perspective *73*
Burns on Johnson *76*
Johnson on Burns *78*

INTRODUCTION

Boxing Day lived up to its name in 1908, when Tommy Burns, the Heavyweight Champion of the World fought Jack Johnson the Coloured Champion of the World, at the Sydney Stadium, putting Australia on the international sporting map and changing boxing forever.

The instigator of the event was the mercurial Australian entrepreneur, Hugh McIntosh, universally known as "Huge Deal" McIntosh following the record-breaking elements of the fight and subsequent film.

McIntosh had developed links with Sydney boxing since 1899, and the announced visit of the American Fleet to Sydney in 1908 prompted him to build the largest open-air boxing stadium in the world. He had met Jack Johnson in Sydney in February 1907 when Johnson beat Peter Felix, and in Melbourne when Johnson beat Bill Lang. Johnson said: "They were really happy days out there. On the first trip in 1907 I knocked out Peter Felix and Bill Lang and made a lot of friends. I also once made a lot of money by accident at Randwick racecourse. I kept lifting my hands to greet friends and the bookmakers took my signs as bets on a horse that. won. If it hadn't won I would probably still be there trying to pay."

McIntosh followed Johnson to the USA and to England to see Tommy Burns fighting. He also saw Johnson call out Burns from ringside in his efforts to secure a Championship fight. Johnson then fought Ben Taylor in England in July 1908.

McIntosh convinced Burns to fight Bill Squires at the Sydney Stadium on August 24, the day the Fleet arrived and Johnson followed Burns to Australia. McIntosh had made £13,600 in gate takings from this fight and asked Burns what he wanted to fight Johnson. When Burns suggested £6000 (about $2 million today), McIntosh agreed. Burns knocked out Bill Lang in September, and Lang would go on to be Johnson's sparring partner for the December bout.

Despite having set up camp with Hattie McClay, the first of many unofficial "Mrs Johnsons", rumours persisted in the press of an affair between Johnson and Sydney woman Lola Toy. The reports of the alleged romance that scandalised Sydney, saw The Referee newspaper sued by Toy for £200 damages in March 1908.

While all odds were with Burns to win, two former Champions—James J. Jeffries and Bob Fitzsimmons—went on the record to say that Johnson would win.

Jeffries had been the Heavyweight Champion who refused to fight Johnson before his retirement in 1905. He had refereed several World titles but declined to referee the match for McIntosh, so finding a referee suitable to both parties was a problem to the day before the fight.

"I finally solved the problem" Johnson stated, "by suggesting that the promoter, Hugh Mcintosh, also a close friend of Burns, should officiate. That really surprised Burns and Co."

With some misgivings, Mcintosh finally consented to act, although "Mcintosh was as nervous as a kitten," said Johnson, "and gave up trying to separate us in clinches after a few feeble attempts. But it didn't matter. Burns was easy, and I had the fight won early."

The event was a spectacular success, the film of the event even more so, as it travelled the world. American novelist Jack London was at ringside on Boxing Day and in his international articles he called on Jim Jeffries to come out of retirement as "The Great White Hope" who would beat Johnson. That fight eventuated on July 4 1910, and Johnson won the so-called 'Fight of the Century' in Round 15.

Over time critics have moved to see that the events of Boxing Day 1908 in Sydney, when the acknowledged Champion of the World was defeated by the skills of a negro from Galveston, Texas, is the true Fight of the Century; a fight against racial discrimination in sport and in life.

Tom Thompson

TOMMY BURNS - Heavyweight Champion of the World

Tommy Burns was the toast of London, Heavyweight Champion of the World - the only problem was that he was being stalked by Jack Johnson, a sharp-talking negro with a growing reputation. Even at ringside, Johnson called for a match-up with little "Tahmmy".

JACK JOHNSON - The Coloured Champion

"Gentleman" Johnson countered with his own postcard series, even sending these to Burns and boxing news editors in Australia, the U.S.A.. England and France.

TOMMY BURNS - HIS FIGHTING METHODS

Burns' book *Scientific Boxing and Self Defence* was published in London in early 1908 by Health & Strength, further antagonising Johnson.

Johnson was in Australia in 1907, and fought Peter Felix and Bill Lang. He sent this postcard to Sydney and Melbourne newspapers.

TRAINING DAYS

TOMMY BURNS TO THE MOUNTAINS

JACK JOHNSON AT THE SEASIDE

Tommy Burns and his good lady wore house-hunting last week. They toured the North Shore in their automobile, and roamed over the various attractive suburbs with which our fine city of Sydney is so closely-hemmed: then they hied them off to the mountains— a nice little party, which Included Mr. and Mrs. 'Jack' Batemen. and Mr. H. Garratt, and during the trip Mr. and Mrs. Burns enjoyed their first pannikin of that peculiarly Australian decoction, - 'billy tea.' "It was glorious," said Mrs. Burns, and she unconsciously smacked her lips at the memory, "and then we had grilled chops— chops broiled on the roadside, fancy that, and I never before thought chops were so nice. What lovely country, too. What beautiful spots for homes, and the delightful homes there are, too. Oh, we have had a great time!"

Every successive locality impressed the world's champion, and a feeling of how happy I could be in any of them took possession of him till the trippers struck Medlow Bath. There was the place indeed. Hilly country galore (Tommy's weakness), and Mr. Mark Foy undertook to fix the great boxer up with a well furnished, detached cottage, having a spacious garden— as attractive a little camp as could be desired, with the fountain baths and other aids to training (including a handball court), ready at hand.

Mr. and Mrs. Burns and trainer Pat O'Keefe leave for their high altitude temporary home to-day, and will not be seen in town again till the date of the big battle— December 26.

Tommy has made arrangements by cable tor Jack ('Twin') Sullivan, who beat Bill Squires In a desperately-waged 10 rounds battle, to come to Australian and assist in his (Burns) training, and Sullivan will be available for matches during his stay, consequently there are some big names ahead In the Stadium proprietary's (Scientific Boxing Mid Self Defence Limited) list, especially an several reputable and well matched local men are to be brought together.

Jack Johnson and suite are located out at the Sir Joseph Banks Hotel. Botany, a resort turnout known the world over in the days of the big pedestrian boom, and a house which has been the training quarters of many a champion athlete, boxers especially.

It was there that Larry Foley, Mick Doolley, Griffo, George Dawson, Billy Murphy, and others of the old brigade attuned themselves for important battles, and there also several of the latter day lot prepared for big successes achieved.

Jack Johnson spent a few days round town calling upon old friends, and shaking the hand of the hero worshipper, who was also much in evidence with requests for the clever black's autograph, and is as strong here as he is in America, which is saying a great deal.

Johnson will got properly under way during the present week with Duke Mulllns as walking pal and rubber down, and, possibly (so 'tis said), Bill Lang as sparring chum; this because Sid Rusnell, through having a fighting engagement on, is not available yet awhile. Johnson put up at the Sir Joseph Banks Hotel when he was in Sydney before, and thinks it, with its delightful surroundings and huge pavilion (13 laps to the mile), where running and walking may be freely indulged in in any weather, and the fine opportunities the district affords for roadwalking, just the thing.

Referee (Sydney), Wednesday 4 November 1908

Jack Johnson training at Botany, some of which was filmed. "We had a lot of fun in Sydney. My training camp was at Botany Bay, and some of the antics we got up to caused many Australians to doubt our sanity. For a bet, I even outran a kangaroo, which dropped dead and tried out my speed running down rabbits. They were good, gay days."

Charles Kerry's portraits of Tommy Burns posing in Sydney a month before the fight at the Stadium.

JACK JOHNSON IN SYDNEY 1908

The December issue of *The Lone Hand* with Norman Lindsay's cover, promoted the fight with articles on Burns and Johnson.

Norman Lindsay's studies of a pensive Tommy Burns.

"BOX ON!"

Norman Lindsay's original drawing of the contestants, November 1908.
Now at the National Library of Australia.

Tommy Burns (rear left) and his wife leave the Hydro Majestic on the morning of December 26 1908.

This original program sold at Lawsons Auctions for $3,100.

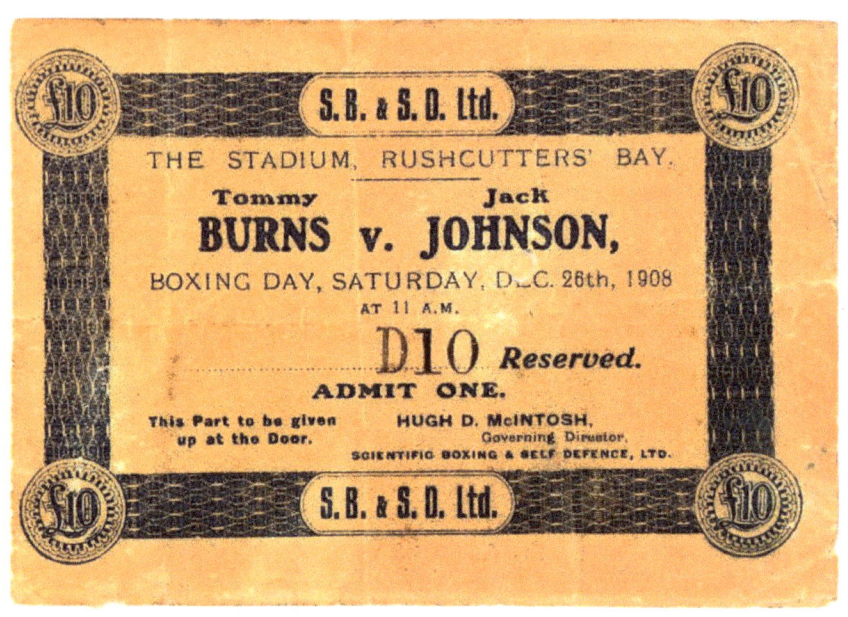

Tickets for the fight were at a premium :
Ringside 10 pounds, then 5 pounds, 3 pounds,
and finally 10 shillings in the bleachers.

SPORTING NOTIONS

The Bulletin, 31 December 1908

The Sydney Stadium is not a place of beauty, but, filled to the rim with 20,000 people, it makes an impressive sight, even to the man who has no interest in the booking office. Saturday's crowd got in without any crushing worth speaking of. Immediately the doors opened at 7 a.m. the early-door ticket holders filed in, and by 8.30 the great enclosure was more than half full. It is said that some enthusiasts slept out near the structure to get in early, but this has been denied as a mere newspaper yarn. The sky was threatening, and in the dark clouds the augurs read an omen of disaster, for that huge crowd was aggressively white in its sympathy. It had not come to see a fight so much as to witness a black aspirant for the championship of the world beaten to his knees and counted out; and though the augurs were persistent, they were voted down. The first excitement was a little affair between photographer Kerry, who had the sole right to take stationary pictures in the Stadium, and some cheerful pirates who had commandeered the platform on which he proposed to erect his big panorama camera. They refused to come down, and when Kerry appealed to the police, they invited the Law to come up and poke them off. The Law said it was no good at climbing. Meanwhile others in the crowd had grasped the value of that eyrie, and proposed to get there. Then Kerry proved his ring generalship. He enlisted the services of the first sec of pirates as a bodyguard against those who were drawing near, and they hoisted him and his machinery up and threatened to kick the heads off any others who attempted to follow.

This little episode over, the crowd leaned back till Johnson suddenly appeared in the passage, and climbing into the ring went to his corner. There was a faint cheer, and the colored giant bowed again and again. He didn't get much homage, but made a lot of what he did get. Then Burns appeared, and was nearly blown out of the Stadium by the crash of applause that thundered from 20,000 throats, for by this time there was not a vacant seat in the great enclosure. Looking round from the ringside over the waves of faces that weltered away to the iron walls of the enclosure, the writer suddenly realised what an awful lot of meat it takes to make up 20,000 people. Johnson was not depressed by the tremendous ovation his rival received. Expectorating with unerring accuracy between the heads of one of his seconds and a pressman on to a vacant space about the size of a handkerchief, he leaned over the ropes and inquired of a menial had he got "that bet on." The varlet had, and Johnson seemed relieved. Then he glanced at the opposite corner, and noticed that the man who was giving him the chance of his life and over two stone in weight, was wearing elastic bands upon his elbows. He demanded that they should be removed. Burns refused. Johnson appealed to the referee, but the McIntosh said there was nothing in the rules against bands, and the agreement had not specified that they should not be worn. Therefore he declined to order Burns to remove them.

"All right," said Johnson, "I'll sit here till he take 'em off. They must be there to do him some good, and if he don't take 'em off there'll be no fight."

Mr. Westmacott announced to the crowd that Johnson refused to fight till Burns removed the bandages, and a storm of howls and hoots ripped the air. Through the bass roar came shrill voices adjuring Burns not to give way to the "black cow," and other animals. McIntosh leaned against the ropes and waited. Larry Foley remonstrated with Johnson, who sat grinning at the rage of the crowd. A man with imagination would have been impressed — he wasn't. Which shows the occasional advantage of not having an imagination. Burns ended what would have soon become an ugly business by suddenly rising and throwing off the thin elastic bandages amidst thunders of applause. Then the official fluter announced that if the police stopped the contest the McIntosh would immediately declare the winner, and that the cheques would be paid over in the ring immediately after the scrap. McIntosh dragged the hands of the two men together, made a few inaudible remarks, and posed them for the picture. Then they went to their corners.

When Burns fought Squires this writer opined that the man who would eventually beat Burns would be one who could draw his defence with one hand and then cross with the other to the jaw. And just because this was precisely what Johnson succeeded in doing at the opening of the struggle, the first round was the really decisive one of the battle. As they came together people got their first chance to realise the great disparity between the men. Johnson's magnificent body and ophidian head and face fairly towered over Burns, who seemed a mere boy in his teens beside him. As Johnson went in he smiled and paused. "Aal right, Tahmmy!" he laughed, shooting out his spar-like left for Burns's ribs. Quick as lightning Burns's right fell on his biceps and took the weight out of the blow, while his left landed in the black man's bingey. As he swung round to draw out they clinched, broke loose, and, like a flash, Johnson, with a tremendous right upward swing, caught Burns fair under the chin, lifted him off his feet, and sent him to the floor in a sitting posture.

This was the really decisive blow of the fight, for, although Burns was not knocked out, he was obviously dazed—so dazed that he lost his ring craft, his hitting power, and his speed. Springing up he went for Johnson like a tiger. But it was blind, dazed fury, which Johnson met with straight lefts and right crosses till Burns at last succeeded in clinching. Then Johnson uppercut him again and again. Burns tried for uppercuts and belly rips, but Johnson had got that far-famed arm lock on him, and Burns's blows had no strength. Then Johnson would push him off and smash him on the jaw as he did so. At the gong Burns went to his corner in a very bad way, and his attendants rubbed him with champagne.

Burns' characteristic attitude.

The black man stood like a tower.

Johnson sat cool and unruffled, laughing and talking. "Water," he roared with a grin, and taking a mouthful that would have been a decent drink for an elephant, he gargled his throat, ejected the fluid where a fair quantity splashed over the furious pressmen, and sat up to have a look at the crowd. He had reason to be pleased with himself.

Not only had he demonstrated that Burns's patent defence was useless against him, but that he was so much stronger that he could hold the champion helpless till he was ready to smite. In his corner, Burns's attendant was combing his hair, and up aloft the cinematograph man went on turning his handle mechanically with an expression of blank indifference, except when he turned his face towards the grey, cloud-covered sky. The crowd sat silent, wondering what the second round would be like.

Johnson cake-walked to meet Burns, who came in determinedly and landed a few useless blows on the black, ophidian face. Excepting that Burns seemed to have recovered some of his speed and showed wonderful skill at evading some right swings, crosses and other messengers of sudden death, the second round was not much better than the first. The audience sighed as it realised that Burns and Jahnson were not in the same class. Someone remarked that Charlie Mitchell was up against greater odds in weight and size when he drew with John L. Sullivan; but an aged fighter sadly shook his hair and remarked that Mitchell didn't lead for the big man's head. Burns got into clinches again, and the towering black held him helpless. He would rise on his toes and bring his right down with an awful smash on Burns's kidneys, then push him off and uppercut him on the jaw as he did so. The referee had a busy time parting them; and once Johnson held Burns with his left and hit him with his right, receiving a warning for his pains. In the clinches Burns's characteristic attitude was one of absolute helplessness, Johnson defending his stomach and avoiding uppercuts with the greatest of ease. A more one-sided struggle it would be impossible to imagine.

Burns was plucky as a lion, but the black man was as strong as a locomotive. The only bright feature of the display was the heroism with which Burns took his smashing, and gamely came again and again. His face was in a very bad way. His mouth was bleeding, his cheek beginning to swell, and his eyes were growing puffy. He seemed to realise his inability to make an impression on Johnson, who occasionally stood quite still, with his hands down, talking and jeering at him, while Burns skirled round looking for an opening that never came. The black man stood like a tower, and let Burns do the fighting. He had evidently read Burns's book.

"I thought Tahmmy was an in-fighter."

It was not till the fourth round that Burns sufficiently recovered from that first knock-down punch to make a really dangerous attack. Then he caught Johnson over the heart with a heavy left, and hauling off landed him a weak right on the jaw. Johnson was quieter for the rest of that round, but it was his round all the same.

Then commenced a most beastly exhibition of rubbing it into a man who was fighting a game battle but was altogether over-matched. The colored mass was quite unruffled, and determined to impress the fact on this crowd of white trash whose champion he was beating. Looking down at a photographer who was snapping between the ropes, he remarked as he went by: "Did you get that? Anyhow, I'll give you a good picture"; and with that he suddenly sprang in on Burns, smote him in the stomach with the left, smashed him on the jaw with the right, and hurled him against the ropes. Frequently he would hold Burns helpless against him whilst he exchanged gibes with the crowd, grinning as he did so, and then twist Burns into the position he wanted and smite. "Come on, leedle Tahmmy," he laughed in the ninth; "come right here where I want you!" and he swung the struggling white into the Johnsonian corner, where Burns broke loose and feebly uppercut. "No good, Tahmmy!" guyed Johnson, "I'll teach you!" and he threw Burns off and uppercut him twice with his right, and bashed him on the side of the head with the left. Again, when McIntosh ordered Burns to break, the white man was too dazed to hear, and feebly jabbed his opponent in the stomach. "Let go - break, Tommy!" roared McIntosh. "He can't hurt, he can't hurt!" sniggered Johnson, bashing Burns over the kidneys. On another occasion, when Burns's seconds howled to him, "Get away from him, Tommy; get away from him!", he drew the white man in close to him, and turning to the corner, remarked, with a drawl, "I thought Tahmmy was an in-fighter."

Burns made a fine rally.

In the 10th round Burns made a fine rally. Feinting with his left, he suddenly hurled in a right for Johnson's jaw with all his weight behind it. Johnson tried to meet it with his left, missed, but ducked in time to let the white man's blow go over his neck. As their bodies crashed together Johnson gurgled : "Ah, that's what I like," and he smashed Burns heavily in the ribs with his right. After 11 rounds of this Burns was in a horrible plight. His face was all puffed out on one side, his jaw hung down as though it were broken, and the blood oozed from his battered mouth. Out-generalled, over-reached, over-matched in strength, insulted and treated like a helpless mouse by a great black cat, he came up heroically to take his punishment. He would fight to the bitter end, and all that a man could do in the face of such overwhelming odds and in the midst of utter disaster. Noah Brusso did. And all the time he continued to attack, to lead, to try and force the fight. It was magnificent, but it wasn't pugilism, and all against the tactics laid down in his own book.

And all the time the cinematograph man up above went on turning his handle monotonously, unexpectant; only glancing at the sky with one eye while he kept the second on his stops. Every time the sinking champion went to his corner his attendant combed his hair. He might lose his championship, the supremacy of the white race might go to the Devil, Burns himself might be slowly battered to pieces or suddenly killed out-right, but at least he should die with his hair properly parted. Gradually the strain began to tell on that attendant and he did his work badly, so that the exhausted, half-fainting man came into the ring with his hair imperfectly parted and badly arranged. The black conqueror was beginning to wonder if he hadn't played too long. He rushed in and at last seemed to be making a genuine effort to end it. But Burns, marvellous to relate, seemed to be slowly recovering his speed, and evaded wonderfully. If he had been content to evade it would have been better if not well, but he continued to lead and meet rush with rush, to clinch, and in-fight; in all of which proceedings he got the worst of it, till he became quite helpless and clung to the ropes. That left side of his face puffed out further, and the sag in his mouth firmly convinced people that the jaw was broken. Johnson also apparently thought so, and, in accordance with the charming spirit he had shown right through the fight, aimed for it every time, as he followed Burns up with sudden ferocious rushes.

It was in one of these rushes that Johnson, while Burns clung to the ropes, struck the champion twice on the apparently injured spot, and knocked him down with such force that he rolled over twice. McIntosh bounded across the ring, and bending down over him commenced to count. Johnson, who all through, although ungenerous and objectionable in his attitude towards his opponent, fought with scrupulous regard for the rules, retired to his corner, and with his hands resting on his hips watched complacently. He thought it was a knock-out.

Johnson thought it was a knock-out.

As McIntosh counted, he waved time with his right hand, forefinger extended, just as Nathan does. "One—two"—right on to eight, when Burns scrambled up and staggered towards Johnson. Johnson bounded from his corner like a panther. "Finish him, Jack!" yelled his second as Johnson swept down like a cyclone on the staggering, almost helpless man, and with a left smash on the forehead knocked him against the ropes. He was just swinging his right for that battered, swollen cheek again, when the Superintendent of Police soared up the ropes and waved his crop aloft. "Stop, Johnson!" bellowed the McIntosh in a voice fit to wake the dead, and Johnson's arm swung back as the attendants swarmed into the ring. Johnson hurried to the centre, and McIntosh, pointing to him, roared, "I declare Johnson winner on points!"

As McIntosh's voice rebounded from the walls of the Stadium that mighty concourse remained silent. Johnson waved his hands to the crowd that did not cheer him. A few straggling voices were raised, but they were mere flecks of sound in an ocean of silence. The black man had fought a scrupulously fair fight, and won on points from start to finish. To the writer it seemed that he could have knocked Burns out any time after the seventh round. But the victory, fairly won as it was, was wholly unpopular. That crowd was white to the core. It had given the brown man a fair deal, and didn't feel called upon to do more. It put its hat on and streamed out. In 12 minutes from the paying over of the cheques the Stadium was empty.

Crowds leaving the Stadium, avoiding the Mounted Police.

"D.": Not the least depressing feature of Saturday's massacre was the "flashness" of Johnson.

"Flashness " is miserably inadequate as a description of his posturing, but it serves as well as the next word. The English or any other language is incapable of doing justice to the way in which Johnson published his delight in himself and all that was his to so much of the world as was at the Stadium. Had I his nods, becks, wreathed smiles, etc., occurred in America, a prominent citizen would inevitably have risen impressively somewhere about the close of the fourth round, and, amid encouraging cheers, have drawn a gun upon Johnson and shot that immense mass of black humanity dead. In the ensuing murder trial counsel for the defence would have put in the cinematograph film as his sole exhibit and evidence, and on its testimony alone secured a verdict of "justifiable homicide."

Boxing Day at Sydney Stadium, with Kerry's camera team on the elevated stage.

The view from the bleachers, 10/- seats, from the same panorama as above.

JACK LONDON ON THE FIGHT

FAMOUS NOVELIST'S ACCOUNT

GRAPHIC PICTURE: CHARACTERISTIC REFLECTIONS

WRITTEN BY SPECIAL ARRANGEMENT, AND TELEGRAPHED FROM SYDNEY

Jack London, author of *The Call of the Wild*, *The Sea Wolf*, and *The Game*, recently reached Sydney, and was present at the Johnson-Burns fight. This is his description of it:—

Full credit for the big fight must be given to Mr McIntosh, who has done the unprecedented, and had the nerve to carry it through. But equal credit must be given to Australia, for without her splendid sport-loving men not a hundred McIntoshes could have pulled off the great contest of Saturday.

The stadium is a magnificent arena and so was the crowd magnificent. It was managed by that happy aptitude which the English have for handling big crowds. The spirit of the stadium crowd inside and out with its fair-minded and sporting square-ness was a joy to behold. It was hard to realise that those fifty or sixty thousand men were descended from the generations that attended the old bare-knuckles fights in England where partisan crowds swarmed the ringside, slugging each other, smashing the top hats of the gentlemen promoters and backers, and swatting away with clubs at the heads of the poor devils of fighters whenever they came near to the ropes.

Never in my life have I seen a finer, fairer, and more orderly ringside crowd, and in this connection it must be remembered that the majority were in favour of the man who was losing. That many thousands of men could sit quietly for forty minutes and watch their chosen champion hopelessly and remorselessly beaten down and not make the slightest demonstration is a remarkable display of inhibition. There is no use minimising Johnson's victory in order to soothe Burns's feelings. It is part of the game to take punishment in the ring, and it is just as much part of the game to take unbiassed criticism afterward in the columns of the press. Personally, I was with Burns all the way. He is a white man, and so am I. Naturally I wanted to see the white man win. Put the case to Johnson. Ask him if he were spectator to a fight between a white man and a black man which he would like to see win, and Johnson's black skin will dictate a desire parallel to the one dictated by my white skin.

But now, to come back to the point. There is no foolish sentimental need to gloss over Burns's defeat. Because a white man wishes the white man to win should not prevent him from giving absolute credit to the best man who did win, even when that best man was black.

"ALL HAIL TO JOHNSON"

All hail to Johnson!' His victory was unqualified. It was his fight all through. in spite of published accounts to the contrary, one of which, out of the first six rounds gives two rounds to Burns, two to Johnson, and two with honours evenly divided. In spite of such mistaken partisanship it must be acknowledged by every man at the ringside that there was never a round that was Burns', and never a round with even honours.

Burns was a little man against a big man, a clever man against a cleverer man, a quick man against a quicker man, and a gritty, gamey man all the way through. But all men are not born equal and neither are pugilists. If grit and gameness should win by the decree of natural law then Burns, I dare to say, would have won on Saturday and in a thousand additional fights with Johnson he would win. But unfortunately for Burns, what did win on Saturday was bigness, coolness, quickness, cleverness, and vast physical superiority.

From any standpoint the fight between Cripps and Griffith last Wednesday night was a far better contest. The men were evenly matched and the result was in doubt from round to round and from moment to moment. And this delicate balance was due to their being equally matched. Each man had opportunity to show the best that was in him. That opportunity was denied Burns.

Bear with me a moment. I often put on the gloves myself, and take my word for it, I am really delightfully clever when my opponent is a couple of stone lighter than I am, half a foot or so shorter than I am, and about half as strong. On such an occasion I can show what I've got in me, and I can smile all the time, scintillate with brilliant repartee and dazzling persi-flage, and in the clinches talk over the political situation and the Broken Hill trouble with the audience. But, Heavens! Suppose I were to don the gloves with Burns, I could no more show what I had in me than Burns showed against Johnson.

That is the whole fight in a nutshell. The men were so unevenly matched that Burns was barred from showing anything he had in him — with the exception of pluck. Johnson was too big, too strong, too clever. Burns never had a show. He was hopelessly outclassed, I am confident that, had a man from Mars been present at the ringside witnessing his first tight he would have demanded to know why Burns was even in the ring at all.

It's hard talk Tommy, but it is no harder than those wallops you received on Saturday. And it is just as true. It is no dishonour to be beaten in a fair fight. You did your topmost best, and here's my hand on it, and on all your pluck and grit and endurance. And Jack Johnson, here's my hand, too. I wanted to see the other fellow win, but you were the best man. Shake.

FIGHT WAS A GOLDEN SMILE

The fight. The word is a misnomer. There was no fight. No Armenian massacre would compare with the hopeless slaughter that took place in the Stadium. It was not a case of too much Johnson, but of all Johnson. A golden smile tells the story, and the golden smile was Johnson's. The fight, if fight it can be called, was like unto that between a colossus and a toy automaton; it had all the seeming of a playful Ethiopian at loggerheads with a small and futile white man, of a grown man cuffing a naughty child; of a monologue by one Johnson, who made a noise with his fists like a lullaby, tucking one Burns into his little crib in sleepy hollow; of a funeral, with Burns for the late deceased and Johnson for the undertaker, grave-digger, and sexton.

Twenty thousand men were at the ring side, and twice twenty thousand lingered outside. Johnson, first at the ring, showed in magnificent condition. When he smiled a dazzling flash of gold filled the wide aperture between his open lips. And he smiled all the time. He had not a trouble in the world. When asked what he was going to do after the light, he said he was going to the races. It was a happy prophecy. He was immediately followed into the ring by Burns, who had no smile whatever. He looked pale and sallow, as if he had not slept all night, or as if he had just pulled through a bout with fever. He received a heartier greeting than Johnson, and was the favourite with the crowd.

It promised to be a bitter fight. There was no chivalry nor goodwill in it, and Johnson despite his care-free pose, had an eye to the instant need of things. He sent his seconds insistently into Burns's corner to watch the putting on of the gloves, for fear a casual horseshoe might stray in. He examined personally Burns's belt, and announced flatly that he would not fight if Burns did not remove the tape from his skinned elbows.

"Nothin' doin' till he takes 'em off," quoth Johnson. The crowd hooted, but Johnson smiled his happy golden smile, and dreamed with Ethiopian stolidity in his corner. Burn s took of the offending tapes, and was applauded uproariously. Johnson stood up and was hooted. He merely smiled. That is the fight epitomised — Johnson's smile.

The gong sounded, and the fight and the monologue began. "All right, Tahmy," said Johnson, with exaggerated English accent, and thereafter he talked throughout the fight when lie was not smiling. Scarcely had they mixed, when he caught his antagonist with a fierce upper-cut, turning him completely over in the air, and landing him on his back

There is no use giving details. There was no doubt from the moment of the opening of the first round — the affair was too one-sided. There was never so one-sided a world's championship fight in the history of the ring. It was not a case of a man being put out by a clever or lucky punch in the first or second round. It was a case of a plucky, determined fighter, who had no chance for a look in at any single instant of the fight.

There was no fraction of a second in all the fourteen rounds that could be called Burns' — so far as damage is concerned. Burns never landed a blow. He never dazed the black man. It was not Burns's fault, however. He tried every moment through-out the fight, except when he was groggy. It was hopeless, preposterous, heroic. He was a glutton for punishment, and he bored in all the time.

MUCH "MOUTH-FIGHTING"

But a dewdrop in Sheol hid more chance than did he with the giant Ethiopian. In all justice, it must be urged that Burns had no opportunity to show what he had in him. Johnson was too big, too able, too clever, too superb. He was impregnable. His long arms, his height, his cool seeing eyes, his timing and distancing, his foot-work, his blocking and locking, and his splendid out-sparring, and equally splendid infighting kept Burns in trouble all the time. At no stage of the fight was either man ever extended.

Johnson was just as inaccessible as Mont Blanc, and against such a mountain what possible chance had Burns to extend himself? He was smothered all the time. As for Johnson, he did not have to extend. He cuffed and smiled; and smiled and cuffed. And in the clinches he whirled his opponent around so as to be able to assume beatific and angelic facial expressions for the benefit of the cinematograph machines.

Burns never struck a body blow that would compare with Johnson's, nor a cross, nor a straight, nor an uppercut; while, as for kidney blows Johnson's most frivolous and pensive taps were like thunderbolts as measured against Burns's butterfly flutterings in that painful locality

Johnson frivolled with Burns throughout the fight. He refused to take Burns seriously, and, with creditable histrionic ability he played the part of a gentle schoolmaster administering benevolent chastisement to a rude and fractious urchin.

The mouth fighting on the put of both men must have seemed bizarre to the Australian audience. Nevertheless mouth fighting as a ring tactic has won more than one battle. But Saturday it neither won nor lost anything. Burns's remarks failed to ruffle his opponent's complacence in the slightest: while there was no need for Johnson's airy verbal irritations, for Burns was as angry as could be from the stroke of the gong. And though Johnson proved a past master in the art of mouth fighting, even his pre-eminent ability in that direction failed to make Burns angrier by one jot or tittle.

There was, however, one result from the word-sparring — an unfortunate result to Burns. He was fighting desperately, and his last hope lay in making the big negro lose his head. Instead he nearly lost his own by having it punched of. Not that he irritated Johnson in the least by what he said. Far from it. Johnson never ceased smiling when the uncomplimentary remarks were addressed to him. Nor did he cease smiling as he proceeded to wallop the naughty boy for his impertinence.

But wallop him he did, in so smiling and summary a fashion as to take the steam out of Burns's verbal punches. In fact, after two distinct adventures of this sort, Burns concluded that the tactic was too disastrous, and abandoned it.

JOHNSON PLAY-ACTED

Not Burns, but Johnson, did the in-fighting. In fact, the major portion of the punishment he delivered was in the clinches. At times he would hold up his arms to show that he was no party to the clinch. Again, he would deliberately, and by apparently no exertion of strength, thrust Burns away and clear of him. And yet again he would thrust Bums partially clear with one hand and upper-cut him on the face with the other. And when Burns instantly fell forward into another clinch, thrust him partially clear and repeat the upper cut

Once he did this five times in succession, as fast as a man could count, each upper-cut connecting and connecting savagely. But principally in the clinches Johnson rested, and smiled, and dreamed. This dreaming expression was fascinating. It seemed almost a trance. It was certainly deceptive, for suddenly the lines of the face would harden, the eyes glint viciously, and Burns would be frightfully hooked, swung, and upper-cut for a bad half-minute. Then the smile and the dreamy trance would return as Burns effected another clinch.

At times, too, when both men were set, Johnson would deliberately assume the fierce, vicious, intent expression, only, apparently, for the purpose of suddenly relaxing, and letting his teeth flash forth like the rise of a harvest moon, while his face beamed with all the happy care-free innocence of a little child

Johnson play-acted all the time. His part was the clown, and he played with Burns from the gong of the opening round to the finish of the fight. Bums was a toy in his hands. For Johnson it was a kindergarten romp. "Hit here, Tahmy," he would say, exposing the right side of his unprotected stomach. And when Burns struck, Johnson would neither wince nor cover up. Instead, he would receive the blow with a happy, careless smile, directed at the audience, turn the left side of his unprotected stomach, and say, "Now here, Tahmy," and while Burns hit as directed Johnson would continue to grin and chuckle, and smile his golden smile.

One criticism. and only one, can be passed upon Johnson. In the thirteenth round he made the mistake of his life. He should have put Burns out. He could have put him out. It would have been child's play. Instead of which he smiled, and deliberately let Burns live until the gong sounded.

And in the opening of the fourteenth round the police stopped the fight, and Johnson lost the credit of a knock-out.

But one thing remains. Jeffries must emerge from his alfalfa farm and remove that smile from Johnson's face. Jeff, it's up to you. And, McIntosh, it's up to you to get the fight for Australia. Both you and Australia certainly deserve it.

BOXING CHAMPIONSHIP
JOHNSON VICTORIOUS
BURNS COMPLETELY OUTCLASSED
A BITTER CONTEST
(by OUR SPECIAL REPORTER.)

SYDNEY, Saturday.- Jack Johnson, the heavy-weight boxer, is now champion of the world. Today, at the Stadium, he met Tommy Burns, the former champion. The fight lasted 14 rounds, and in every round, Johnson completely outclassed Burns, who received terrible punishment so much that in the fourteenth round the police stopped the fight, and the referee Mr. H. D. McIntosh, declared Johnson the winner. Johnson was unmarked. Burns hail never succeeded in getting a blow home.

There was an immense crowd inside the Stadium, and a still greater crowd thronged the streets outside, and swarmed up telegraph poles and on every spot from which a glimpse of the ring could be obtained. Johnson, attended by five seconds, including Bill Lang, the Victorian, was the first to enter the ring. He was received with mingled cheers and hoots, for the crowd were eager for the victory of Burns. Besides this, Johnson's bombastic talk had created a warm feeling against him. He had loudly proclaimed to everybody his certainty of defeating Burns, and looked on the fight as an easy triumph for him. "I'm going to the races Saturday afternoon, sure," he told everybody. "Little Tammy's going to spend his Saturday afternoon in bed." So the crowd hooted him.

When Burns came through the Stadium into the ring, there was a storm of cheers. For five minutes the crowd yelled itself hoarse. When the cheers died down inside the Stadium, they were taken up by the thousands outside. It was as though some giant echo had been awakened. Burns wore a very serious expression. It was plain that he recognised the strength of Johnson's claims to superiority, but he looked cool and determined, though, in marked contrast to the jaunty, smiling confidence of Johnson. Johnson came into the ring wearing a grey bath-robe. Burns was dressed in an old blue suit, and a battered green felt hat. Johnson wore a grey cap. The inevitable suitcase accompanied Burns, and his clothes were quickly peeled off and put into it. Then he, too, put on a bath-robe, and the men were nearly ready.

AN INITIAL HITCH

There were the usual preliminaries, and challenges, mid announcements. Dr. Maitland examined the gloves and weighed them. They were 4oz. each, with most of the weight in the wrist and palm. The men put on the gloves, and Mr. McIntosh called upon them to start. Johnson threw off his bath-robe, and stepped out from his corner, but as he did so he caught sight of Burns, also stripping. Burns was wearing elastic elbow-bandages. Johnson drew back into his corner, and sat down, with his bath-robe huddled round his shoulders.

"No! no!" he said. "He must take them off; he must take them off. No! no! Ile mustn't wear those."

Burns had stood up, but he sank back into his chair, with an air of resignation and a shrug of the shoulders. Johnson's seconds appealed to the referee. Mr. McIntosh inspected Burns's armbands.

"They are all right," he said to Johnson. 'You will have to go on."

But Johnson sat where he was, saying to himself, "No! no! He will have to take them off."

Just before this the crowd had started a chant to cheer Burns to fight:

"Good boy. Tommy; good boy, Tommy,"

Ten thousand throats were shouting it, with a cadence in it that made it sound like some tremendous battle-song. At this unexpected halt of the boxers, the chant died away thinly, and a wondering silence followed.

The official announcer called through a megaphone from the four sides of the ring: -"Johnson refuses to fight unless Burns removes his armbands. The referee declares that the armbands are allowed." The whole audience seemed to be hooting - an angry, vicious hooting which meant trouble for Johnson, as it appealed likely that the fight was not to commence.

Johnson paid no attention to the hooting, monotonously muttering, "No! no! He must take them off." Burns remained impassive in his corner, and his looks said plainly that he was determined not to remove the armbands. Then Mr. Larry Foley was called into consultation. His verdict was that the armbands were against the rules, bul that they could not possibly benefit Burns, and that Johnson was foolish to persist in his objection.

The problem was solved by Burns, who rose and indignantly ripped off the offending bandages. Again he received its ovation from the crowd.

After that there was nothing to delay for. The men posed for photographers, went to their corners, and the gong sounded for fight to commence. Not a moment was lost by either man. Johnson seemed hilariously happy. Burns, in his well-known crouch, danced up to Johnson, who towered over him. Johnson weighed just 14st., and Burns just half a pound over 12st. Burns looked like a small boy beside the beautifully-modelled giant. Johnson stood in the centre of the ring like a great bronze statue as Burns danced up to him. Burns sparred at the gigantic figure for a moment. Johnson winced. "Come on, Tahmy," lie said, "you've got to get it' and the statue woke to sudden violent life, as he stepped in, finishing his left on to Burns's ribs. Here was a chance for Burns to use his skill at close quarters. It had been supposed by everybody that Burns would beat him at in-fighting but Johnson, with quick flashing blows, reached Burns's ribs, and then, withdrawing his right like lightning, sent it crashing back in an upper cut which sent

Burns to the floor. The fight had not listed a quarter of a minute, and Burns was down he stayed on the floor for six seconds, and as soon as he rose Johnson bore down on him again, firm-footed, wary, cool and smiling. Burns rushed in and clinched. There he tried to adopt the tactics which have stood him in such good stead before smashing in vicious blows on the ribs, and reaching up lo the jaw wherever possible, but Johnson's defence was superb. Whenever Bums hit Johnson's glove fell lightly on his biceps and pressed the arm back so that the blow had no power. Johnson stood straight up smiling while Burns, with head down, pounded away at his ribs. As he smiled the negro said softly, "Ah poor little Tahmy" He Ieaned over Burn's bent head, and drove his right down to his kidneys, again and again, then he straightened again, murmuring 'Dont you know how to fight, Tahmy? They said you were a champion." Then they separated only to clinch again while Johnson amused himself by stiffening his abdominal muscles, and letting Bums punch at them

It was obvious to everybody that Bums was a baby in his hands. Johnson was too strong, too tall, too heavy, too skilful, and a far better ring general than his opponent. It was plain too that they hated each other, and every blow had in it the sting of bitterest spite. Yet both were too skilled as boxers to do anything approaching foul fighting. About the middle of the first round, which was packed so full of incident and wonder that it seemed lo last for hours, Burns shot an upper-cut on to Johnson's chin but Johnson merely smiled in answer. It had not hurt him. "Now, Tahmy," he said and his face set into fierceness as he sent right and left to Burns's body; and then with another stinging uppercut Bums was knocked down again, but he sprang to his feet instantly. Burns had discovered that he was over-matched. He grew careful. He saw that his only chance of winning lay in snapping an opening for a knock-out blow. That opening never came. Johnson, whenever he chose, forced the fighting. In that first round he again and again perplexed Burns by a murderous looking feint with his left hand, followed instantly by the right crossed on to the side of his face. The left side of Burns's face began to swell from the hail of blows. The spot

Johnson had chosen was high up on the jaw, too high up to knock Burns out, and it seemed even then (it grew certain later on) that Johnson had made up his mind to keep Burns in the ring as long as possible, and punish him as much as he could while all the time he taunted him.

JOHNSON'S GREAT STRENGTH

Burns jumped lightly out of his corner for the second round, and feinted at his opponent. Johnson had taken up his statuesque pose with the light hand low down across his body, and the left swinging loosely from the shoulder. The giant left forearm, however, was used as a bar of bronze, all the muscles standing out tense on it. It was the same with his right when he used it. He did not hit with his fist only, but with the whole of that tremendous, rigid forearm, propelled like a battering ram at ins on opponent. Johnson laughed at Burns's feinting.

'That's right, Tahmy, feint away; you'll fight directly, perhaps," he leered and dropping his fists, he stood up in attitude of indolent arrogance daring the white man to come on then suddenly he stepped forward and lashed out at Burns with those terrible fists. Burns clinched, and again the pair struggled in holds. Johnson using his great strength with such practised ease that the efforts of Burns seemed puny and childish It might have been a good-humoured father allowing his son to cling to his waist and batter at his ribs, knowing well that the boy's little punch could not hurt him. Burns brought all his skill into play, but he could not penetrate Johnson s defence. Johnson coolly turned his blows aside with his glove and took the force out of them in striking him on the biceps. Burns gave up the attempt to fight at close quarters, and took to long range fighting. But he soon found that his opponent was equally his master there. Johnson simply stood still Iel Burns feint and sluice at him until an opening came; then with a paralysing rush he would dash at Burns, driving his left hand in to the body, crossing with his right and aiming blows with such strength and fury that Burns could only defend himself by clinching, and accepting punishment at close quarters.

In the third round it was the same. Whenever he liked Johnson seemed able to hit Burns wherever he liked. The crowd felt that Burns needed comforting. They started the battle song:

"Good boy Tommy; good boy Tommy."

BITTER TAUNTS

Perhaps Johnson did not like the adulation of Burns. At the beginning of the fourth round he called out, "Come on Tahmy; come on and fight" and moved over to Burns. Burns glared at him, and snarled from between his swollen lips, "You cur." Johnson did not smile, "Huh," he said, and Burns paid for his remark, Johnson flew at him and forced him across the ring with powerful blows on the body, sending in a fierce upper-cut as they clinched and then smashing him on the swollen spot in the face again and again as Burns clung to him. Then he posed again, immovable while Burns danced round him, only to be driven back as Johnson bore down on him. The fourth round ended with Burns showing unmistakable signs of weariness. He struggled slightly as he returned to his corner. His body was cut and bruised all over where Johnson« terrible hammer blows had been filling. The left side of his face was bulging, his lips were swollen, his eyes blackened. Johnson was smiling fresh, and cool, and, if possible, more confident than ever.

Burns recovered wonderfully during the minute interval but the next round sent him back to his corner worse than ever. Johnson was playing with him like a great cat playing with a mouse. Burns was completely at his mercy but he did not knock him out. He was showing the crowd who had hooted him how immeasurably superior he was lo the man they cheered. Johnson kept up a running fire of taunts. Burns had gained a great reputation as a fighter at close quarters and Johnson made a point of this.

"I thought you were an in-fighter," he would leer.

"Don't you know a lot about it?"

"Oh yes. You're a champion in-fighter all right."

Every jibe was punctuated by a vicious blow, twisty upper-cuts which seemed irresistible, right and left swings lo the body, and hard jabs in ribs and face. Then he would rest awhile; Iet Burns struggle and hit, while he glanced round the crowded Stadium, laughing and flinging remarks to his seconds and friends. He was terrible in his insolence. By the sixth round, after driving Burns all round the ring, lohnson said:

"Say littie Tahmy, you're not fighting. Can't you? I'll have to show you how."

Then he stood off for a moment, only to pounce upon Burns again with a terrific blow on the ribs.

"See it," he cried and glanced over at his corner. One of his seconds signed him to watch Burns, and not look out of the ring so much, but Johnson smiled contemptuously.

"I see him, oh, yes, though he is so small,' he jeered.

"JEWELL WON'T KNOW YOU."

Burns was showing indomitable courage. He had no chance in the world now Johnson had proved conclusively that Burns could not knock him out, and every minute Burns stayed in the ring seemed only to bring him more punishment for his bruised body and his puffed-out face must have been causing terrible pain. But he showed no sign of giving in. He was there to fight till he dropped if Johnson persisted in his evident resolve not to knock him out. His other cheek, the right, was cut by the seventh round, but it did not swell up. Johnson was reaching his face mostly with his right hand and it was the left side which received most of the blows. In the seventh round, in the middle of some fierce fighting in a clinch, Johnson gazed serenely over Burns's head, and said to the crowd as Burns vainly belaboured him on the ribs, "He can't hurt. I thought Tahmy was an in-fighter."

Burns was clinging to Johnson a good deal, Johnson raising his hands in the air to show that it was not he who was holding on. But he always kept one hand ready to guard against any sudden blow from Burns, and those came frequently enough, vicious uppercuts, which might have brought Johnson down had they struck him fairly. He was too quick, however, and always saved himself with a heavy counter blow, perfectly timed or flicked Burns's glove aside as though it were a fly. At the end of the seventh round Johnson swung his long left arm on to the side of Burns's head, and sent him to the floor. Burns was up in two or three seconds, but the blow had told and Burns clinched to save himself from another attack. At long range Johnson was treating him badly, but the gong came to Burns's rescue with its minute's respite.

As the round opened it looked every time is though Johnson was going to finish the fight there and then, but this was merely his craftiness.

He knew that Burns was freshened up with the minute's interval, and fanning and sponging, and it was his plan to weaken him again at once. So he commenced vigorously, and then, as Burns weakened again, adopted his attitude of contemptuous superiority.

"Come on now Tahmy," he said, as he opened the eighth round, "Jewel won't know you when she gets you back from this fight."

He sent in crashing blows with both hands.

"Did you see that one?" he exclaimed, is he poked his left glove softly on to Burns's mouth, and drove a terrific right cross on to the white man's swollen cheek. They clinched, and Burns managed to force his right on to Johnson's mouth. It was not a painful blow, but it dyed the negro's gold teeth with red. Johnson grinned widely but he watched Burns very closely during the rest of the round, though he never ceased his gibing talk. At the end of the round he patted Burns on the shoulder and said. "Poor little boy." Burns turned round and made a grimace at him. It was pathetically ridiculous. The champion of the world had been reduced to grimacing. Johnson saw it and smiled contentedly. It indicated to him how weak Burns must be.

TERRIFIC PUNISHMENT

"Are you going to fight, Tahmy?" asked Johnson for the hundredth time, as they met. at the beginning of the ninth round.

"Yes, you big dog," almost wailed Burns.

"Sure! But don't cry over it," replied Johnson, as he hurled Burns back with a fearful blow on the ribs.

"I'll teach you something," went on Johnson.

"Look at this, and this,"

"And this."

Every word was accompanied by brown flashes, which descended in blows from right and left on Burns's body and face. If Burns protected his face the blow reached his body. If he guarded his body it reached his face. It was the supreme science of boxing. Burns was helpless before it. When Johnson ceased Burns clinched. Tho negro smiled whimsically. As he looked over him, and said, "You're a great lighter, aren't you, Tahmy?" Burns was sorely distressed, but he broke away from his opponent, and dodged across the ring, leading at him with fierce lunges, then dancing back quickly before the smiling black could reach him.

His next round - the tenth- brought only more punishment for Burns. Johnson seemed really in earnest; he followed Burns round the ring using both hands with terrible effect. Burns had become mechanical in his fighting and nothing but his splendid footwork saved him from a knock out. A dozen times Johnson sent home terrific blows on Burns's face and stomach, but Burns was moving away just at the moment of impact, and did not drop. The eleventh round showed Burns at his best. He was then horribly disfigured by the punishment he had received. One side of his face was frightfully swollen, the other side cut and bruised. He could only speak with difficulty. Still, he seemed full of vigour. Successfully concealing the deadly weakness which must have been gripping him, he tried several times for knock-out hits, but Johnson's heavy countering robbed them of effect. At last, Burns darting out of a clinch, got a heavy right swing home on the side of Johnson's head, and awoke the cheers of the crowd, who had been singularly silent during the last few rounds. After that Burns led freely, and forced the fighting, but Johnson never let him get home a blow again. Burns staggered to his corner when the gong sounded and it seemed certain that the next round would see him counted out.

It was obvious in the twelfth round that Burns was beaten, and many of the spectators, tired of seeing him uselessly battered, began to inquire, "Where are the police." But Burns fought on, enduring Johnson's insults, and taking the fearful punishment served out to him without flinching. Only now and then he hissed through his bruised lips "You cur" and every time he did so Johnson smashed his heavy right on to Burns distorted left check. In the clinches, as had been the case all through, Johnson seemed able to uppercut Burns whenever he pleased.

Burns has a superstition that 13 is his lucky number, and his seconds cried to him, "It is your lucky round," as he left his corner for the thirteenth round. The luckiest thing that could have happened to him then was to have been speedily knocked out, but this was no trait of

Johnson's plan. He had clearly made up his mind to work off all his old scores on Burns. Burns was very weak. The spring had gone out of his footwork. He held his arms as though the gloves weighed pounds instead of ounces but Johnson had no mercy. He did not try for the chin, but instead he let Burns spin and clinch for a while then jumping in he smashed his left three or four times lo Burn's ribs, which were raw with the battering they had received. Then he directed his attention to Burns's face and sent in a series of savage uppercuts, whose effect could be judged by the way they jolted Burn's head back. Johnson was almost holding Burns up when the gong sounded and Burns staggered to his corner. His "lucky" round was over.

POLICE STOP FIGHT

The fourteenth round was not finished. The calls for the police to stop the fight had been becoming more and more insistent, as it was realised that Johnson was merely cruelly playing with Burns. When the round opened the two men sparred for a few seconds. Johnson seemed to measure carefully his distance for a moment, then he smashed, rushed in, and drove his left straight into Burns's face, following it with his right on the swollen cheek half a dozen times in quick succession. Johnson hit with all his powers first with the light and then with the left. It was only the rapid succession of the blows, first on one side, then on the other, which kept Burns on his feet. They clinched, and as they broke away Johnson sent out his left and light again, and this time Burns went down. He stayed eight seconds on the floor and rose. Already Dr Maitland had spoken to the police inspector, and the inspector was walking to the ring. Before he reached it the two men came together again, and Johnson pelted in another series of heavy blows. But the inspector was in the ring. The referee stopped the men, and declared Johnson the winner. It was only a limiter of seconds and Burns would have been down again almost at once, and it is inconceivable that he could have avoided a count out - he was completely exhausted.

There was no doubt about Johnson's overwhelming superiority. He made Burns look like a novice. He had an advantage of 5in in height and 1in in reach, and this, of course, stood him in good stead; but Burn's forcing and hitting power, wonderful is they are, cannot be compared with Johnson's. He dealt with Burns just as he dealt with Lang on the Richmond racecourse in 1907. But he set out to punish Burns, whereas he let Lang down as lightly as possible. Burns had previously drawn the colour line against him, and only last Thursday had insulted him with having "a yellow streak." From the time they stepped into the ring until the fight was stopped Johnson bore these things in mind.

However poor a showing Burns made as a boxer and hitter, he proved himself a man of extraordinary pluck and stamina. His capacity for taking punishment is something altogether remarkable. His gameness is beyond question. He never once wavered or flinched all through those fourteen rounds, while he took without a quiver blows that would have counted out any other man. The punishment he inflicted on Squires in Sydney four months ago was a mere bagatelle beside that which he received today. He had taken every means lo help him to success. His training had been sound and careful. A code of signals on the same line as American baseball signals had been arranged with his seconds, who could be heard during the fight calling "Twenty-three," "Thirty-five," "Twenty-six." All the code words gave him some particular secret instruction but with all this, from the time he was knocked down 10 seconds after the fight began, only his immense courage and determination enabled him to stand before his skilful, powerful, pitiless antagonist.

In a front row at the ring side sat Mr Jack London, the well-known American author and his wife. No lady has ever been admitted to an important fight in Australia before; but it was known that Mrs London was coming and a half a dozen ladies were also present in parts of the Stadium. One wore a boxer hat, probably to appear as much like a man as possible in the cinematographic picture.

The fight was an unusually bloodless one, but it was also unusually fierce.

Johnson waiting for Burns to get up from the canvas.
A rare hand-coloured photograph by Charles Kerry.

JOHNSON INTERVIEWED
WANTED TO GIVE BURNS A BEATING

Jack Johnson did not want to be worried by interviews. He was unmarked and unwearied, and supremely happy. "I guess anybody who wants to interview me has got to come right out to my place at Manly," he said, "I am busy now." His people were crowding into his dressing room. "Get some policemen to keep that door clear," he called and half a dozen constables were bought to guard the entrance. Johnson, however, withdrew his embargo, and graciously permitted the police to admit the interviewers. He smiled broadly as his trainers rubbed him down. "Say, I guess I gave Tahmy a beating he'll remember, " he said 'Oh, yes, some of them have been saying about me being yellow, having yellow streak, and all that sort of thing. I guess little Tahmy looked as yellow as I did. When I got him in the ring I made up my mind what I was going to do with him. I knew I would win, but I figured out to give him i beating he was not likely to forget in a hurry. I whipped him proper, and I did it on purpose. I wanted to beat him down bit by bit and show him and the public how much 'yeller' there was in me. Tahmy's a game, straight fighter all right but he did not give me as much trouble as Bill Lang gives me in training. I could have won a long way sooner only I wanted to beat him proper so's he'd remember me," and Johnson laughed a delighted laugh. "Yes," went on Johnson, "Squires challenged me today. He can have a fight for £2,000 - that is if he still wants it," and again Johnson chuckled.

BURNS AFTER THE BATTLE
"I'M THROUGH WITH BOXING"

Sydney, Sunday. Burns was very badly marked in the fight but he sustained no serious injury, no injury, that is to say, which is considered serious by a pugilist. His splendid physical condition will enable him to recover completely in a few days.

When interviewed a few hours after the fight Burns seemed very happy and cheerful, though he looked as though he had fully earned his £6,000. He said – "I did my best; but Johnson was too big and too strong. Although I scaled 12 stone and half a pound on Friday, the morning before the fight I was only 11st 1.1/4 1b, to that I should have been in a lower division than Johnson. I gave him the chance to win the championship because of a promise made early last year that I would fight him as soon as I had disposed of all the top-notch white fighters in sight. I need not have done so. The colour line was drawn very rigidly by the white champions before me, and I could have followed their lead. When I signed to meet him I knew what I had to face. I knew his skill, size, and strength. Although I reckoned he was the toughest proposition I had been up against, I thought I might win.

"So Johnson is exulting, is he? Well, that's nothing to his credit. He s beat a man half-a-foot shorter than himself and 2st lighter. Men who ought to know tell me that he scales every ounce of 15st and not 13st 10lb, as was announced. Don't I say I'm making excuses. I was only showing that there isn't any reason for the big fellow to throw bouquets at himself. Had he been any ways near my poundage and height I guess there wouldn't have been any new champion today.

"About the fight? Well, that punch in the first round rattled me, and I never fully recovered from it. I screwed my ankle, too and that interfered with my footwork. I let the trouble spell for a bit, and then tried to liven things up, but it hurt too much. I don't know what I am going to do in the future, but I can tell you one thing, I'm through with boxing, and no one is more pleased than Mrs. Burns. There's no one in sight with a chance against Johnson. He is sure to hold the championship for a long while if he looks after himself

"I intend to reside in Australia, and become an Australian citizen. This will be my home. I will live amongst friends for whom I have a warm affection and I feel sure that I will be welcome."

LARRY FOLEY INTERVIEWED

One of the onlookers at the ringside in the Stadium was Larry Foley, a champion heavyweight of some years ago, and the instructor of many of the best boxers the world has seen. Mr Foley was interviewed after the fight was over, "Well, you saw it," he said "and what can you say, except that it was all one-sided. Burns was not strong enough, not big enough, not clever enough. He had not a hope. He is a good natural fighter, you see, and he is not very clever. Yes that's right. He beat Squires and Laing and Roche and Moir and the others, but if you could do a hundred yards in twelve seconds, and all the other men you had to race could only do it in fourteen seconds, you'd look like a champion sprinter, you see, but what would you look like when a man who could do it, in evens - in ten seconds came along. Well, he would make you look slow, wouldn't he? Burns met his ten seconds' man today, and we found that Tommy was only a twelve seconder. That's it, all right. He is a good middleweight. I won't even say that he is a champion middleweight He's a good plucky, natural fighter with a hard hit, and some good foot work, but he is not in the same class as Johnson, who has length, weight, reach, strength, cleverness, and brains. You don't want much more, you see.

"It was the worst championship fight I've ever seen, and I have seen a good few," Mr Foley went on. "Burns never laid a finger on Johnson. You might say the big fellow was too clever, too wise. But Tommy showed great pluck. He took punishment like a man, all right. It's funny that a fighter as poor as Tommy could have ever been champion of the world. He struck a barren spot in the history of boxing when there weren't many good men about, and he had the luck, or the good sense to miss Johnson up to now you see. Johnson, in my opinion, will hold the championship for a good while, until someone a bit better than himself crops up. Jeffries? Yes, perhaps. Well, that's all about it. You don't need to know about fighting to see that Tommy was beaten out of sight. That first hit in the first round ended it all, as far as he was concerned, and Johnson could have hit him any time he wanted to."

Argus (Melbourne) - Monday 28 December 1908

THE BURNS-JOHNSON FIGHT - THE FILM

Biograph pictures of the struggle between Burns and Johnson will be almost immediately sent through the: States of Victoria and South Australia, accompanied by a complete series of the training pictures of the two champions as they appeared daily in their preparations at Medlow Bath and Botany respectively. It is understood that Mr. Spencer, the operator of the Lyceum Theatre, Sydney, was eminently successful in his efforts to secure a fine picture of the contest, and from a private view each blow could be readily seen. These pictures are likely to prove a great attraction throughout the States. The management has decided to charge popular prices. The pictures will be seen at the Adelaide Town Hall on January 8, 9, and 11. Mr. Allan Hamilton has secured the sole rights of the famous fight picture, likewise the training pictures, from Mr. H. D. McIntosh, governing director of the Scientific Boxing and Self-Defence Limited, Sydney, and he wishes it to be particularly well known that only one film will travel the two States. Mr. Hamilton will be represented on the tour by Mr. George Buller.

Register (Adelaide), Monday 28 December 1908

The Referee's specialist W.F. Corbett wrote a 70 page coverage in early 1909.

A $40,000 Dollar Contest with an earning Capacity of $1,000,000
BY MEANS OF
THE WORLD'S
Heavyweight Championship Pictures

Between TOMMY BURNS and JACK JOHNSON
(WORLD'S CHAMPION)   (COLORED CHAMPION)

"DEFENCE!"

Taken from all four sides of the ring simultaneously, in the presence of 30,000 people, at **THE STADIUM,** Sydney, Australia, on Boxing Day, Dec. 26th 1908.

Made under Australia's "clear-cutting" sun at high noon, under conditions insuring the highest perfection in moving picture art.

Showing the different training tactics of each contestant, Motor Car Pacing, Swimming, Rabbit and Kangaroo Chases, Tree and Mountain Climbing, Physical Exercises, Bag Punching, Massage Treatment, Sparring, Arrival at Ringside, The Crowds, View of the Approaches, The Interior, Preparations, Final Instructions, The Gong, **The Climax.** Views Afterward. **Making in all two hours of unsurpassed realism.**

WORLD'S RIGHTS NOW OPEN
. . . TO NEGOTIATION. . . .

Australia, New Zealand, The Phillipines, China and Japan India and Straights Settlements already disposed of.

FIRST TIME IN THE WORLD'S FISTANIC HISTORY . . . . .

That the Champion Representatives of the White and Black Races has met for RACIAL and INDIVIDUAL Supremacy, since cinematographic pictures became a fine art.

Cable——
HUGH D. McINTOSH   -   Proprietor
PERMANENT ADDRESS—
Challis House, Sydney, Australia,
Until January 22nd, and after September 15th, 1909.

TEMPORARY ADDRESSES—
Cecil Hotel, London, Feb. 8th to 15th, 1909.
Majestic Hotel, Paris, Feb. 16th to 22nd.
C/o English Consul, Berlin, Feb. 23rd to 27th
C/o American Consul, Christiana, March 1st to 5th
Knickerbocker Hotel, New York, after March 12th, 1909.

Hugh D. McIntosh, Sydney, Australia

"POISED."

Advertisement in Corbett's *Burns & Johnson in Australia*.

THEATRE ROYAL
HOBART

ENORMOUS ATTRACTION.

3 NIGHTS ONLY 3
SATURDAY, MONDAY & TUESDAY
JANUARY 16 18 AND 19

ALLAN HAMILTON'S
BIOGRAPH TOUR
of
The World's Sensation

Which took place at Sydney, December 26th

PRICES. 3s. 2s. 1s.

WORLD'S GREATEST PICTURES,

showing graphically, accurately, realistically

World's Greatest Fistic Event.

The GAUMONT CO. Ltd., Sole Agents for U. Kingdom.

ONLY Moving Pictures taken of

BURNS-JOHNSON FIGHT,

illustrating—

- Botanical Gardens, Sydney.
- Burns in Training.
- Burns' Garden Party.
- Burns Swimming.
- Medlow Baths, Australia.
- Botany Bay, Australia.
- Johnson's Full Training.
- Excitement of Ticket Selling.
- World's Biggest Fight Stadium.
- The Early Morning Crowds.
- The Rush for Admission.
- The Stadium — 20,400 Spectators.
- Panorama of Spectators.
- Every Detail of Great Contest.
- Burns and Johnson in Ring.
- Johnson's Refusal to Fight.
- Argument between Seconds.
- Johnson's Deadly Uppercut.
- Burns Knocked Down.
- Johnson Jesting with Spectators.
- Burns' Desperate Rallies.
- Burns' Damaging Ankle Sprain.
- Every Blow Struck.
- The Police Interference.
- Johnson declared the Winner.
- Paying over the Huge Cheques.
- No Detail Omitted.

Declared by Press and Public to be
"FINEST PICTURES EVER TAKEN."

These Pictures of the World-Famous Contest for the Championship of the World.

NOW BEING EXHIBITED AT

Royal Court Theatre,

SLOANE SQUARE, S.W.

Evenings, 7.30 and 9.

MATINEES: Wednesday and Friday, 3.
Thursday, 2.30 and 4.30.
Saturday, 2, 3.30, 5.15.

PRICES.

EVENINGS: Stalls, 5/-, 3/- and 2/-; Dress Circle, 3/- and 2/-; Upper Circle, 1/-; Pit, 1/-; Gallery, 6d.

MATINEES: Stalls, 2/6 and 1/6; Dress Circle, 1/6 and 1/-; Pit, Upper Circle and Gallery, 6d.

Children under 12 half price.

4 DAYS ONLY! Commencing Wednesday, March 31st.

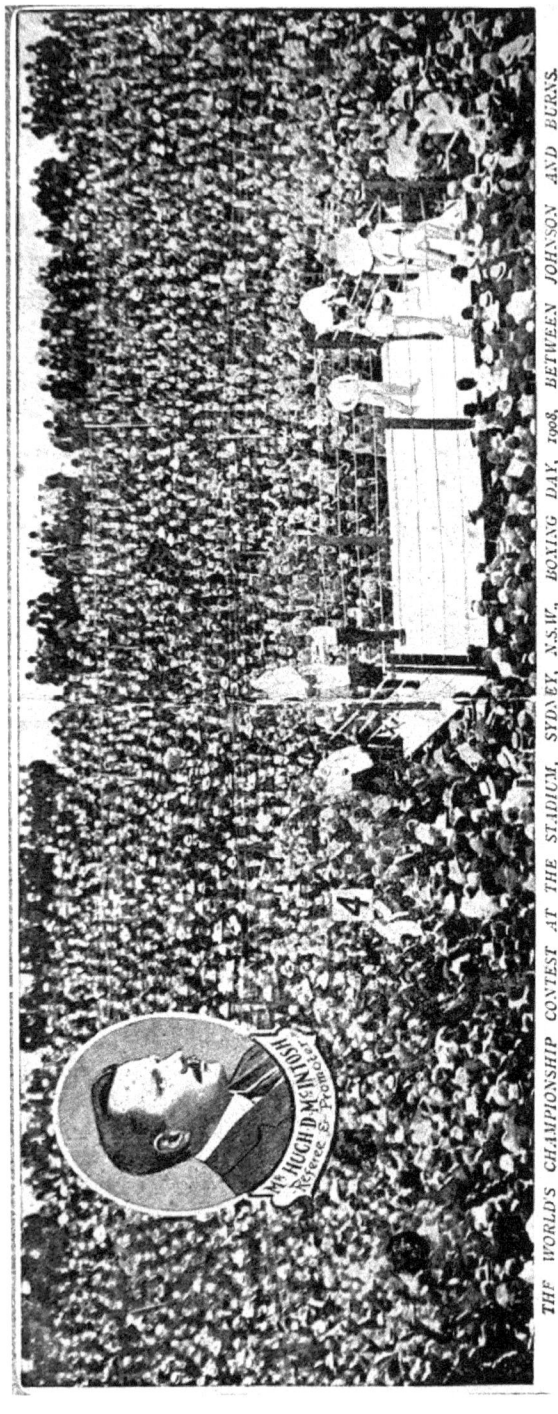

THE WORLD'S CHAMPIONSHIP CONTEST AT THE STADIUM, SYDNEY, N.S.W., BOXING DAY, 1908, BETWEEN JOHNSON AND BURNS.

THE GREATEST FISTIC EVENT OF HISTORY! PURSE: Winner, £1,538. Loser, £6,212.

FACTS OF THE FIGHT.

WINNER. Jack Johnson, Galveston; height 6 ft. 0½ in., weight 14 st. 7 lbs. **LOSER.** Tommy Burns, Canada; height 5 ft. 7 in., weight 11 st. 12½ lbs.
STADIUM. 480 ft. by 360 ft. (app. 4½ acres); 2,000 tons of timber used; cost to erect (app.), £2,600; time to build (night and day shifts), 6 weeks.
STAFF. Employees, 244; police 250; mounted police, 150; also 250 Pressmen representing every leading paper in the world.
RECEIPTS. Advance booking, £10,200 (a world's record). Total Gate Receipts, £26,500 (another world's record). From training exhibitions, £2,000; from advertising, hoardings, and souvenir, £2,100.
PICTURES. "The Bonanza of the Fight: Success Tests Credulity." Cost of taking picture in triplicate, £1,500; 15,000 ft. of film used for negatives only. 10,000 photographs of various incidents during the fight sold within one week. Receipts of picture exhibitions to date over £30,000. Estimated value of pictures based on offers received, £75,000. 500,000 ft. of films leased up to date.
SOME PICTURE TAKINGS. Melbourne (1 week), £1,737 19s. (1; Sydney (18 performances), £3,158 17s.; Brisbane (7 performances), £1,761; Adelaide, (10 performances), £1,027 18s.; New Zealand (9 performances), £1,111 12s. Unexampled record.
SPECTATORS. 20,400 paid admissions; 40,000 outside Stadium. Gates opened at 6 a.m.; 10,000 seated by 7.30 a.m.; at 8.30 only £3 seats left for sale. Thousands turned away from gates; not one seat vacant at time of contest. 40,000 people handled in six hours without mishap or confusion.

COPYRIGHT.

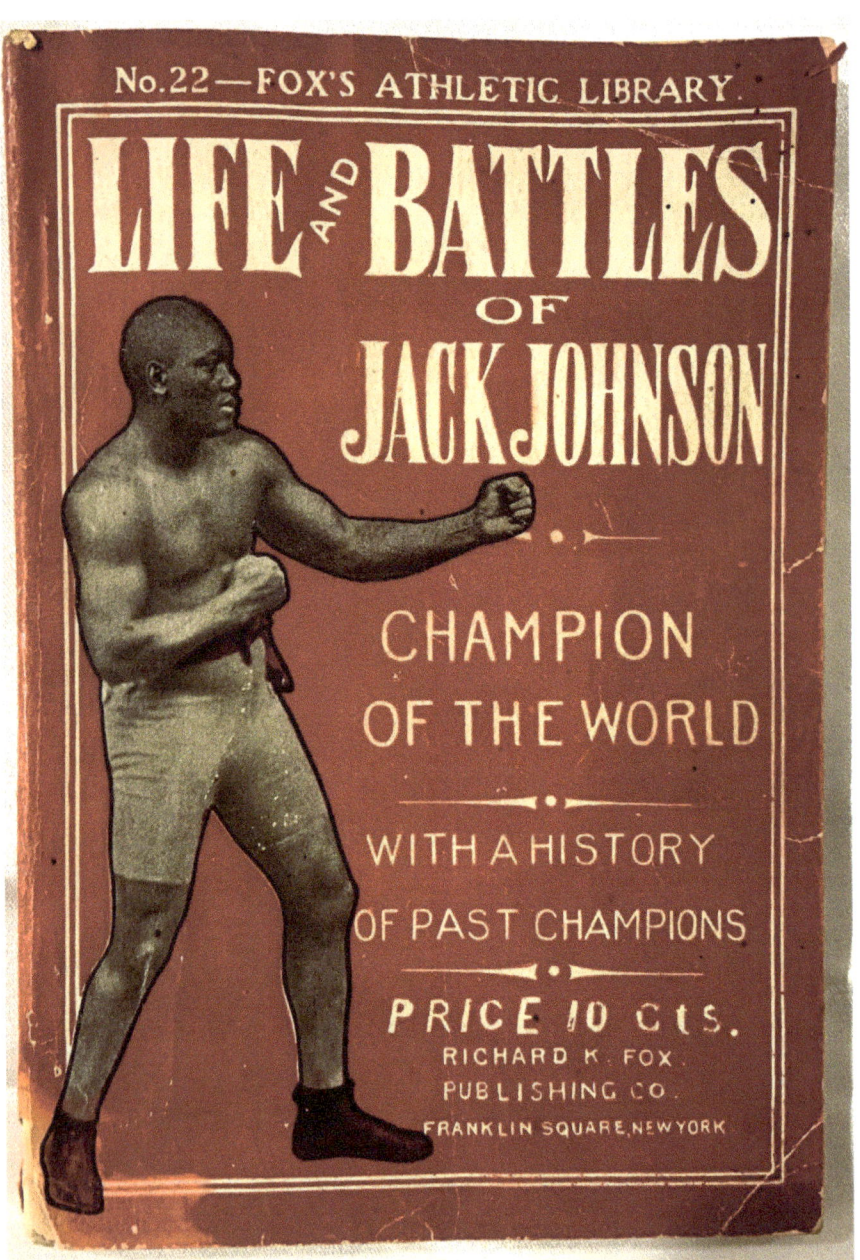

THE BATTLE BY ROUNDS
An American View

First Round. — After a few moments of preliminary sparring Johnson reached Burns with a sharp upper cut and the Canadian went to the floor, remaining there for the count of eight. He signalled to his seconds that he was all right, however, and when he arose sailed in for Johnsons body. Johnson swung a hard right to the head, and Burns staggered backward nearly across the ring from the impact of the blow. Then Burns, rushing in, planted a right of great force on Johnson's chin and by an excellent display of boxing warded off a return. Johnson, nevertheless, managed to put through a stinging left to the head at the sound of the gong.

Second Round. — When the gong clanged Johnson yelled across to the approaching Burns, "Come right on," and he swung his right and landed hard on Burns' chin. The champion's ankle gave way under him and he went down, he was up immediately, however, and Johnson got to close quarters with him and placed right and left to face and body. Burns' left eye here commenced to swell. Johnson thus far had the better of the battle.

The big black man was coming all the time and he swung a terrific left into Burns' stomach. Burns was doing but little. He was bleeding from the mouth and apparently was tired. The men were clinched as the bell rang.

Third Bound. — Burns swung his right to Johnson's head and then did some wonderful execution at infighting, chopping his right to the ribs frequently. Johnson during the round landed some terrific blows to the kidneys.

Fourth Round. — When the men met in the centre of the ring Johnson shot a heavy right into Burns' ribs. The men talked wildly to each other, each seemingly intent upon getting the other excited and landing the money winning punch. During the jeering they sparred fiercely, but few blows were struck. Then Johnson swung left to the body and Burns brought right to head. Johnson, closing in, threw a terrific right and left to the head of the Canadian. The bell found the men in a hard clinch.

Fifth Round. — Apparently refreshed from his minute's rest, Burns started the round briskly, landing his right on Johnson's head and punching the body with both hands. Johnson managed to slip over a few rights to the head during the round.

Sixth Round. — Johnson rushed and Burns clinched. Breaking loose, however, with one hand, Johnson swung his right a dozen times into the white man's ribs. Burns jolted Johnson's body frequently and swung his right hard over the ribs and put a stilt left to the stomach several times. Johnson treated these blows as a joke, laughing at the crowd and making sarcastic remarks to his opponent as be bustled Burns into a corner and scored a couple of rights to the body.

Seventh Round. — Johnson rushed Burns across the ring, dealing out rights in which there was no mercy. Burns got a left to Johnson's jaw and Johnson raised a lump under Burns' right eye in return. Burns here seemed to be losing strength. Johnson was landing repeatedly on Burns' eye, meanwhile addressing the people about the ringside, and though Tommy was working dexterously at infighting he placed several terrific blows on Burns' ribs, dropping him to the floor for a few seconds.

Eighth Round. — Burns' eyes were puffed up and he was bleeding from the mouth when he emerged from his corner. The white man's blows apparently had little effect on the Texan, who went severely about belaboring the head of the champion.

Ninth Round. — "Come on. Tommy; swing your right!" yelled Johnson as the gong rang. Burns responded by calling the negro a "yellow dog." There was not very much fighting, probably more talking, during this round.

Tenth Round. — Both men seemed tiring. Johnson still used his fists effectively on Burns' head and stomach and Burns was doing all he could in reply. His blows, however, lacked steam.

Eleventh Round. — The perspiration pouring off the body of Johnson made it look not unlike highly polished walnut. Burns tried to cross his right over, but Johnson cleverly avoided him, meantime laughing at the champion.

Burns is outclassed and Johnson apparently is invulnerable. When the bell rang Burns limped to his corner.

Twelfth Round. — Johnson continued to rush and Burns took a tremendous lot of punishment gamely. His jaw is greatly swollen.

Thirteenth Round. — Johnson continued to play for the injured eye and the cut mouth of Burns, which was swollen twice its normal size. Blow after blow the colored man rained upon him, and the gong alone saved the white man from defeat, for he was reeling and groggy as it rang.

During the intermission between the thirteenth and fourteenth rounds the police officials consulted together, and it seemed probable that they would stop the fight in the next round. Mcintosh went to Burns' corner and had a talk with the champion, who declared that he was strong. Mcintosh then asked the police not to interfere.

Fourteenth Round. — Johnson went right after Burns when time was called. The white man warily backed away, but Johnson, following him up, dropped Burns with a heavy right to the head. "One, two, three," slowly counted the referee, and Burns remained down until eight seconds had been tolled off. When he arose Johnson flew at him like a tiger, and, using both hands unmercifully, soon had the champion tottering. The police then jumped into the ring and stopped the fight.

Hugh D. McIntosh, the referee, immediately declared Johnson the winner, he added that he considered it the best fight he ever had witnessed in Australia and that both men had fought most fairly.

from *Life and Battles of Jack Johnson,* Richard K Fox 1912

BURNS ON JOHNSON

Dec 7th 1953. Coalinga California U.S.A. Box 566

Dear Bill O'Loughlin, your letter 25/10/53 received I was very pleased to hear that Bill Squires is in good Health inclosed find a clipping of Bill Squires & myself in the Coalinga Record two days ago, it will explain itself, what I am doing today as you requested, I am healing the sick and the suffering with the power of thought qualified with Love through the Cosmic Consciousness as Jesus did 2000 years ago and as He is doing today.

My contest with Jack Johnson Dec 26-1908, reminds me that in all my previous Contests I had used the secret of relaxation during all my rest periods, but at the time, race prejudice was rampant in my mind. The idea of a black man challenging me of the white race was beyond endurance. with that ruling my consciousness I went out to Bill. I surely did hate which was the opposite to relaxation, thus I was tense and unable to defend myself — Johnson was the very opposite and naturally won this contest, I however, was fortunate in not being hurt, I was not bleeding although I had a swollen jaw.

Johnson held no hate against me. To prove that this was born out years later when I was operating a night club in New York. Johnson was broke when He came into my club and asked me if I would and I know now he was a great teacher and not an opponent and I realize the Ward Christmas means freedom and to love is freedom.

Jack Johnson has received help from me since he has passed on, as all people who pass on live in the same consciousness as they did while in the flesh body while on the earth plane, as the parable of the rich-man states, who wanted a drink of water to quench his thirst. Enclosed find photo taken a few days ago, and my card which you may publish with the article anywhere except Canada or U.S.A.

With love universal to Australia
always your friend in christ-love
Tommy Burns

In 1953, Tommy Burns has a Cosmic acceptance that Jack Johnson was "a great teacher and not an opponent" in this letter to Bill O'Loughlin.

JOHNSON ON BURNS

In 1909 in Vancouver, B.C., Johnson told a crowd of people that Burns deserved credit as the only white heavyweight who ever gave a black man a chance to win the title. He said, "Let me say of Mr. Burns, a Canadian and one of yourselves, that he has done what no one else ever did, he gave a black man a chance for the championship. He was beaten, but he was game."

Effect of the fight - Aboriginals boxing at Barambah, December 1908.

www.ingramcontent.com/pod-product-compliance
Lightning Source LLC
Chambersburg PA
CBHW050820090426
42737CB00021B/3453